Eight Things Every Man Should Know about Depression

By

GARY H. LOVEJOY, PHD

AspirePress

Peabody, MA

AspirePress

Eight Things Every Man Should Know about Depression
Copyright © 2017 Gary H. Lovejoy
All rights reserved.
Aspire Press, an imprint of Hendrickson Publishers Marketing, LLC
P. O. Box 3473
Peabody, Massachusetts 01961-3473 USA
www.HendricksonRose.com

Book cover and layout design by Axel Shields.
ISBN: 9781628624113

Contents

PART 1:

PURPOSE, PATTERNS, AND PRECONCEPTIONS OF DEPRESSION

Chapter I

The Meaning of Depression

> **The first thing every man should know: Depression is an alarm signal to tell you that certain issues need attention so that they won't keep damaging you.**

"I'm upset to be here," a forty-two-year-old insurance salesman said. "But my wife said if I refused, she would take the kids and leave." As John saw it, his life was out of control. Everything was going haywire and he couldn't stop it. He hated his job and detested his boss.

What's more, he could never seem to please his wife. His children "went around him" to get what they wanted from their mother. "Nobody respects me. All they do is use me. I'm a paycheck to my wife, an ATM machine to my kids, and a scapegoat to my boss. I'm sick and tired of it."

Though he still loved his wife, it angered him that she was always unhappy with him about one thing or another. He resented her for turning the kids against him. He had come from a broken family of origin, and he didn't want to lose his own family.

It didn't help that he had few friends and no one with whom he could share his feelings. The closest he came to a friend was complaining to the bartender at a local bar. He thought coming to counseling was an admission of failure—and likely a waste of his time.

When I suggested that he was profoundly depressed, his eyes widened. He protested that he knew he was angry, but he didn't think he was depressed. When I described the characteristics of depression, he acknowledged he fit the profile. He'd thought depression was passive withdrawal, indicating a person too emotionally weak to handle stress.

DEPRESSION AS A USEFUL ALARM SIGNAL

What we mean when we use the term *depression* doesn't refer to a day or so where you are feeling the blues—a normal but temporary state of feeling down. A person's emotional state naturally varies, having normal ups and downs that are relatively mild and short-lived. Depression, on the other hand, is a persistent, negatively charged emotional experience that fundamentally changes your view of life.

There are at least a dozen characteristics of depression that include:

1 — Overwhelming feelings of emptiness and hopelessness

2 — Feelings of worthlessness and self-hatred

3 — Anxiety and agitation

4 — Loss of interest in almost all activities that used to provide pleasure

5 — Pervasive fatigue or exhaustion

6 — Various bodily aches and pains

7 — Loss of appetite, or the opposite— out-of-control eating

8 — Problems falling asleep or staying asleep (insomnia), or sometimes sleeping too much (hypersomnia)

9 — Excessive or inappropriate guilt, most of it false guilt

10 — Increased impatience, anger, irritation, and/or frustration

11 — Difficulty concentrating and focusing on the task at hand, often leading to paralyzing indecision

12 — Thoughts of suicide and intrusive fantasies of death

Now consider how severe your depression might be. Here are three categories of depression. Where do you fit?

Major Depressive Episode	You are experiencing at least four or more of the symptoms described on page 8, leaving you incapable of undertaking normal activities and responsibilities.
Dysthymia, or Persistent Depressive Disorder	Your symptoms are milder; you can still function in life, even if unhappily; and you have been struggling with these symptoms for at least two years.
Normal Depression	Your symptoms are even milder—often the result of a sudden and unexpected loss—for instance, losing someone important to you. This type of depression is a natural part of the grieving process and will gradually dissipate as appropriate grief work is done.

In contrast to cases of normal depression, more often depression is a sign that something has gone emotionally awry in your life and requires the healing of your heart and mind. Depression may even indicate a long-standing issue from early childhood.

The fact is that depression is an emotional alarm signal that tells you that you need to attend to something that has damaged you in the distant or recent past and is likely still damaging you in the present. Though it's dreadful to experience, depression is designed to protect you from further damage, which is the true purpose of any alarm signal.

It's in this context that we like to say, "Depression is to the psychological self as pain is to the physical self." Just as pain alerts you to something that has gone wrong in your body so that you can take remedial action where necessary, depression alerts you to emotional wounds that need healing. Depression is emotionally disruptive for a reason: Its intense discomfort gets your attention so that you will get the help you need. In this way, your depression has a protective function and is your *ally*, not your enemy.

> **Depression is designed to *protect* you from further damage, which is the true purpose of any alarm signal.**

God desires that we heal from damage. We need not feel ashamed of such an important alarm signal as depression. Rather, it's far better to see depression as a clarion call to intervention and change, leading us to the emotional healing necessary for a richer, more satisfying life.

Depression directs your attention to repairing emotional damage done to you by events over which you had little control. Depression can get you to address the false self-talk that started with these events and will continue to be destructive until you change it. You are likely as unaware of the lies you tell yourself as the truths that should replace them.

Feeling All Alone

Even if you feel alone, you have a lot more company than you think. Depression affects almost twenty million people in the United States alone and is one of the leading causes of disability worldwide.

What's more, it is no respecter of persons. It hits:

- The rich and the poor
- The educated and the uneducated
- The white-collar crowd and the blue-collar worker
- The young and the old
- Loners and the socially active
- Every ethnic group
- Christians and non-Christians

In their lifetime, most people will experience the struggles of depression—either in themselves or in the ones they love. So you see, you are not really alone. It's just that so many who are suffering depression are ashamed to reveal it. This is especially true of Christians who incorrectly believe that if their faith were strong enough, they would never fall prey to depression.

Yet we get a very different picture in the Bible. Many faithful servants of God suffered depression—even suicidal depression. They were not rebuked for their struggles but, rather, lovingly counseled toward a new perspective, given instructions for renewal, or simply reminded of God's compassionate trustworthiness.

Situation	Scripture
Moses was oppressed by the burden of caring for the complaining Israelites.	Numbers 11
Elijah was despondent after Jezebel threatened his life.	1 Kings 19
David was in despair about enemy attacks, and then writes one of the world's favorite psalms of comfort.	Psalms 22–23
An aging and weakening psalmist was in need of God's comfort, and praised God for his strength and righteousness.	Psalm 71
Jonah was upset that God had chosen not to destroy the people of Nineveh.	Jonah 4
Paul felt great despair and worried for his life.	2 Corinthians 1

THINKING AND DOING
SOMETHING DIFFERENT

Still, there are those who feel guilty about being depressed, as if depression itself is evidence of distrust in God. Or they believe that depression is punishment for sin or a sin in itself. By *sin* we mean the failure to do what is right or to resist God's will. Even if depression is a *consequence* of sin, our depression reminds us that God's forgiveness is how to experience his peace.

It's clear that sin is not a reflection of how strong our faith is: "Indeed, there is no one on earth who is righteous, no one who does what is right and never sins" (Ecclesiastes 7:20). Even a righteous man cannot entirely escape sin. It's a natural consequence of our sin nature. God himself does not expect us to live a perfect life. He asks only that we follow him with our whole hearts and minds despite our imperfections.

"Out of the depths I cry to you, LORD;
Lord, hear my voice.
Let your ears be attentive
to my cry for mercy.
If you, LORD, kept a record of sins,
Lord, who could stand?
But with you there is forgiveness,
so that we can, with reverence, serve you.

> I wait for the LORD, my whole being waits,
> and in his word I put my hope.
> I wait for the Lord
> more than watchmen wait for the morning,
> more than watchmen wait for the morning.
> Israel, put your hope in the LORD,
> for with the LORD is unfailing love
> and with him is full redemption.
> He himself will redeem Israel
> from all their sins."
> — *Psalm 130* —

Even the prophet Isaiah—who was well known for his upright behavior—fell on his face and cried out, declaring himself to be a man of "unclean lips" in the presence of God's impeccable righteousness (Isaiah 6:5). The Christian's shame, triggered by depression, is a sign of a hidden perfectionism that God has already dealt with by his grace.

LIFE IN THE FALLEN WORLD

In addition to our own sin, we have to deal with others sinning against us. When God's perfect world was soiled by Adam and Eve's sin, God knew that a natural consequence would be human suffering. As one pastor put it, "There is no human heart that, if you touch it, won't bleed a little." Suffering is common to us all.

But God's love is displayed at every turn in our lives. He provided a plan for our eternal redemption through Christ's death and resurrection. And the emotional trigger of depression is an alarm system that God embedded within our hearts and minds to tell us we need to mend from the damage wrought by life in a sinful world.

> **The emotional trigger of depression is an alarm system that God embedded within our hearts and minds to tell us we need to mend from the damage wrought by life in a sinful world.**

It's Also about the Journey

God is interested in our eternal destiny and our earthly journey leading up to it. This is witnessed in God's dealings with the people of Israel. His plan for them was to have them settle in the land of Canaan ("a land flowing with milk and honey," Exodus 3:8); but this happy ending occurred only after a disobedient generation had passed away after forty years of tormented wanderings in the wilderness (Numbers 14). Through it all, God never stopped caring for (and taking care of) them, no matter how far they wandered from him.

A purposeful God, he never lets an experience, good or bad, go to waste. This same God is in constant pursuit of you and me, with the same desire to take care of us, even when we cry out in our pain and accuse him of abandoning us.

Wired for Relationships

Looking at how we're psychologically structured, we can see that we are wired for relationships—wired to love and be loved in return. That's why God made relationship the central feature of his plan of redemption.

To summarize the entire Bible in a few words, God is saying to each of us, "You matter to me." This is a reflection of God's own heart. Everything else in the Bible simply validates this point. His death on the cross and his subsequent resurrection provide all the proof necessary that we matter to God.

Because he created us, God knows that, underneath all that we say and do, we have a basic desire to matter to someone—anyone. Let's be honest, men. Most of our achievements reflect this longing to be acknowledged. This is what makes setbacks in our work and careers so significant. A sense of adequacy emerges only when we successfully fulfill the desire to matter or be significant to others.

When men don't feel important—whether to their spouses, their children, their friends, or their bosses—at first they get angry and defensive; but, over time, they inevitably slip into the throes of depression. Without being able to see any purpose to their lives or any meaning in what they do, they feel completely inadequate. Often, they think to themselves, "You should take your troubles like a man and bootstrap yourself up." The stiff-upper-lip approach may sound like the best policy, but it usually denies you the help you need.

> **A sense of adequacy emerges only when we successfully fulfill the desire to matter or be significant to others.**

When you're depressed, nothing makes sense. You see others as cruel and rejecting—even spouses who eventually withdraw or lash out in frustration. In many instances, your life is filled with self-fulfilling prophecies of unrelenting emotional pain.

To the outside observer, you may act in ways that appear calculated to alienate others, and then you lament that no one seems to care. The observer, however, doesn't see the pain underneath the aggressive façade. All they see is the critical spirit and the frightening meltdowns, so they're more than ready to run. But when you're depressed, it's one more betrayal, one more experience of abandonment.

However, there are ways to get unstuck from this perpetual victimhood. But it means stepping back from your usual take on events and considering an entirely different way of thinking. The *inescapable conclusions* you have bought into are not, as it turns out, as inescapable as you may think.

Thinking and doing something different from what you've done in the past can surprise you with unanticipated healing. So you need not abandon the optimism of God's plan for your life after all. Heed the call of depression and you will discover different ways to connect with life, ways that exchange a dreary existence with a new, more hopeful one.

Chapter 2

The Different Faces of Depression

> The second thing every man should know:
> The expressions of depression fall into five
> identifiably distinct patterns of behavior
> determined by emotional associations.

Just as there are different types of physical pain, there are different patterns of symptoms for depression. Some of these patterns often go unrecognized. Furthermore, most people are unaware that patterns of depression tend to be gender sensitive, meaning that men show certain patterns more often, and women show other patterns more often. In order to understand how we internally organize these symptoms, we must first understand the way we make emotional associations.

Have you ever met someone for the first time and, while you're talking to that person, begin experiencing really negative feelings toward him or her, but you don't know why? The reason is usually because the person you're talking to reminds you of someone you had a bad experience with. It could be something in the way that he or she dresses, gestures, stands, makes facial expressions, or uses some other mannerism. The key is that some characteristic or group of characteristics the person is exhibiting triggers a negative emotional association for you.

This can happen without triggering the actual memory. In effect, you are experiencing the emotionally charged feelings separate from the actual memory. So it leaves you puzzled as to why you are feeling the way you are.

Beginning in early childhood, we learn to associate emotions with characteristics of people or situations.

A few examples:

- A man who had a verbally and/or physically abusive father comes to hate authority figures, sometimes even getting in trouble with the law.

- A man whose home of origin was filled with angry conflicts during the holidays becomes frightened and depressed during what to everyone else is a festive time of year.

- A young woman's mother and father had vicious arguments, even fisticuffs, at the dinner table and demanded that the children remain in their seats. The result? She became severely anorexic, associating food with the toxic environment she had grown up in.

After a long history of such hurtful associations, people usually erect emotional walls around themselves as protection from further damage. Unfortunately, these walls also keep out redemptive experiences that could transform their world.

Over time, people with a history of pain develop some of the depressive symptoms described earlier. And they do so according to the particular emotional associations that have defined their life experience. That's why there are different patterns to the array of symptoms displayed in different people.

FIVE PATTERNS OF DEPRESSION

Among depressives, there are certain common characteristics: feelings of helplessness, emptiness, and low self-esteem. There are additional characteristics that fall within five common patterns—described in the checklists below. As you read each characteristic, decide if it applies to you. These lists can help you identify which pattern or patterns of depression best describe you.

Pattern #1: Withdrawn Depressives

- Are often marked by a morose indifference to life and have a kind of resigned quality about them

- Avoid people as much as they can, preferring to be alone

- Reject conversation—are likely to withdraw into a room alone

- Are driven to ruminate on everything negative in their lives

- Engage in repetitive, mentally disengaging, and solitary activities such as vegetating in front of the TV or playing video games for hours

- Teach other family members to *give them space* by telling them to tiptoe past their room, to be quiet, to leave them alone, etc.

"And let us consider how we may spur one another on toward love and good deeds, not giving up meeting together, as some are in the habit of doing, but encouraging one another."
—Hebrews 10:24–25

Michael Card, the well-known Christian singer, described his father, a physician, as a withdrawn depressive. One of his most poignant memories of his father was trying to engage him by getting on his hands and knees and talking to him through the small space under the closed door to the family den. Sadly, his father rarely responded, other than to tell his young son to go away and leave him alone. This type of behavior is easily recognized as depressed. It's the picture most people associate with depression.

Pattern #2: Angry Depressives

- Are generally irritable and angry toward others

- Direct anger toward themselves, especially after having let loose on someone else

- Fill their conversation with a deep pessimism, describing life events with gloom and doom

- Make their home (and sometimes workplace) like a minefield, with everyone waiting for the next explosion

- Are difficult to live with

- Impulsively lurch from rage one moment to regret or self-recrimination the next

- Believe that others make life difficult for them, constantly blaming other people or situations for their troubles

- Have a way of turning happy events into sour experiences

- Are pleased by little

- Create an environment where their family organizes life around them, hoping not to set them off

- Watch or listen to news or talk shows that focus on every negative event, unaware of how further depressed it makes them

Ironically, many times, these individuals are not viewed as depressed but as having an anger problem—which, of course, they do. A large number of people enrolled in anger management programs are, in fact, profoundly depressed. Habitual expressions of anger can be an effective cover for deeper feelings of despair.

I remember a man who closely fit this profile. His wife was afraid of him, so she kept her distance. His sons despised him, fighting with him regularly. Hardly a day went by that he wouldn't complain or lose his temper over something.

However, he would speak despairingly about his family's treatment and how life was a huge disappointment. He repeatedly questioned why so many things went wrong. In some ways, he wanted to give up. But he clung to hope that things would get better, though his gloomy outlook on life often sabotaged that hope.

Pattern #3: Somatic Depressives

- Have obsessive bodily concerns, usually focusing on one particular physical symptom or another, which can shift or change over time

- Traipse from one doctor to another, seeking confirmation that they are afflicted with some debilitating disease

- Are convinced their lethargy, bad feelings, aches, and pains provide an excuse for not participating in life's responsibilities and for creating drama about their health

- Express their depression through their bodies; are often referred to as *hypochondriacs*

- Are in a constant, even desperate, search for some kind of personal significance

- Would rather talk about their physical complaints than discuss their underlying anxiety and depression

- Often have a history of a significant loss or severely stressful event

A while back I treated a very depressed woman who claimed she had chronic fatigue syndrome. She lived with a highly controlling husband who not only made all the decisions but did all the shopping and household chores as well. He didn't trust his wife to do these things to his satisfaction. As a result, she had retreated to her bed, saying she was too sick to muster the energy to do anything.

> "Human anger does not produce the
> righteousness that God desires."
> —James 1:20

One day she vigorously marched into my office, claiming a miraculous recovery. Apparently, her husband had become quite ill and was unable to do any of the tasks he normally did. Essentially, in their marriage, they could not have two healthy people at the same time. With her husband being sick, she was finally free to get up and get going on her day. This is a good example of a somatic depression. It was actually warning her that her marriage was sabotaged by their unspoken bargain to have only one functioning spouse in order to avoid conflicts.

Pattern #4: Dependent Depressives

- Are overwhelmed by intense anxiety, especially relational anxiety

- Constantly appeal to others to be their friend

- Careen from one crisis to another

- Resent feeling helpless and believe that life is out of sync with their abilities or resources

- Seek people out, making incessant demands for help

- Emotionally drain others dry and will entrap their rescuers into a cycle of weariness and false guilt

- Become overwhelmed with panic and accuse their rescuers of abandonment if they step back from the relationship

Pattern #5: Anxious Depressives

- Are constantly worrying about something—typically imagining worst-case scenarios

- Fight extreme feelings of nervousness and fear, believing something catastrophic will happen if they aren't hypervigilant

"For the Spirit God gave us does not make us timid, but gives us power, love and self-discipline."
—2 Timothy 1:7

- Have generalized feelings of anxiety or actual anxiety attacks, where they experience heart palpitations, profuse sweating, shallow breathing, and feelings of impending doom

- Often end up in the emergency room, convinced that they're having a heart attack when they are having an anxiety attack

- Continuously seek reassurance from their spouses and/or friends that something terrible or catastrophic will not happen

- Tend to make heavy use of medications (like Xanax) that are designed to calm them down

- Likely had parents who openly worried a lot and tended to be overprotective

A Common Thread

Anxiety is a powerful component of many depressions. In fact, it frequently precedes depression. It's a signal reflecting a basic insecurity about coping with life's challenges. It often arises from the fear of being emotionally or physically hurt.

People feel especially hurt when they feel they don't matter—that what they think, feel, or believe is invalidated or dismissed as unimportant. While anxiety may be the fear of getting hurt, anger is the most common reaction to actually being hurt. Openly acknowledging our hurt makes us vulnerable, so instead we go on the attack to protect ourselves.

Anxious depressives protect themselves from whatever they consider dangerous and will not relax their vigilance. Depression often arises from desperately trying to ward off every potential harm. If something bad does happen, it is seen as catastrophic. This doesn't leave much to look forward to.

> "But let all who take refuge in you be glad;
> let them ever sing for joy. Spread your
> protection over them, that those who
> love your name may rejoice in you."
> —*Psalm 5:11*

GENDER DIFFERENCES

These various depressive patterns are not gender neutral. Instead, men predominate in some and women predominate in others. Clinical experience has shown that men are more likely to represent the withdrawn and angry depressives, with gender representation about equal among somatic depressives.

Statistics show that about twice as many women report depression as men. And while four times as many men as women successfully commit suicide (largely due to the fact that they tend to use more lethal means, like guns), twice as many women attempt suicide. But statistics can be misleading. After all, if men are less likely than women to be depressed, then why are so many men committing suicide (almost 26,000 per year)?

Suicide Deaths by Gender and Method [1]

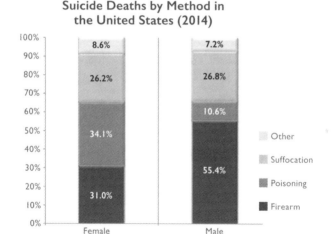

Suicide Deaths by Method in the United States (2014)

Correcting for gender bias, recent studies suggest that the numbers of men and women struggling with depression are possibly closer to being equal. It's just that men do not disclose their symptoms to their physician as often as women do. Men form their identities from being competitive and successful—not vulnerable and emotionally fragile. This interferes with their ability to talk about negative or sad feelings with others.

The Top Two

As stated above, of these five patterns, men predominate in two: withdrawn depressives and angry depressives. Because they are less likely to talk about what they are really feeling inside, even to good friends, the chances are they will either disguise what they feel as anger or withdraw altogether.

You can see this tendency when men avoid being too personal in conversations. If you observe a group of men and a group of women both talking together the differences are striking:

- Men are usually conversing about the latest news in sports, about business concerns, or about politics— all of which are emotionally safe topics requiring little self-disclosure.

- Women, on the other hand, are more likely talking about family matters, their relationships with their

children, or various events that are bothering the—
most of which freely reveal their underlying feelings.

One is relatively impersonal while the other is often
highly personal in nature.

Personal Isolation

In marriage, women tend to look for intimacy and
companionship, suggesting the security of being
emotionally close. Men, in contrast, look for respect and
physical connection, involving more a sense of adequacy.
When couples come in to see me, the wife commonly
reports she feels lonely and unloved, while the husband
bitterly complains that he can never please her. To him,
recognition of his contributions to the relationship seems
to be absent while blame is frequent.

These responses are different because of the different ways
their depressed feelings are expressed. Because depressed
men are more likely to abuse alcohol and other controlled
substances, they prefer to do these things alone to avoid
criticism. This criticism, normally from their spouses,
drives them to be more secretive and wary of detection,
leading to further withdrawal.

On the other hand, men might withdraw during times of
unemployment, when they feel like failures or, in their
later years, when they retire. For many men, retirement

feels like losing their purpose in life or losing a sense of importance and accomplishment. Feeling useless is the last thing a man wants to feel.

While men are only slightly more frequently found among withdrawn depressives than women, they are counted much more heavily among the angry depressives. Their gender bias toward aggressive behavior naturally makes them better candidates for a more agitated depression.

From early on, the socialization process affects boys differently than girls. Girls are trained to tamp down their anger, act in more modest or sedate ways (i.e., being more *ladylike*), and talk things out. Boys, on the other hand, are trained to be more overt in their anger and aggression.

> "Cast all your anxiety on him
> because he cares for you."
> —I Peter 5:7

Such socialization teaches that aggressive expressions of anger are more *masculine*. In similar fashion, girls get the message that acting out their anger is *unfeminine*. As studies confirm, men put fewer limits on their anger whereas women more likely view anger as being counterproductive. In both cases, however, anger and depression produce a heavy pessimism about the prospects for a happy life. This pessimism saturates their conversations and drives their behavior.

Since power and control issues frequent men's concerns, they often display their bad feelings through irritability, contentiousness, and undisciplined rage. Their frustrated and blaming demeanor (including self-blame) leads to outbursts that push their wives and friends further away. The result is more isolation.

Little wonder that the suicide rate for men is as high as it is. It's also another reason why men typically do not fare as well emotionally after divorce as women do. Despite all their bravado, men do not adapt to marital dissolution with the independence women do.

Two Years after Divorce[2]

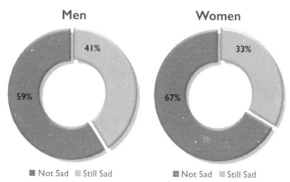

Men / Women

Men: 41% Still Sad, 59% Not Sad

Women: 33% Still Sad, 67% Not Sad

■ Not Sad ■ Still Sad   ■ Not Sad ■ Still Sad

Likewise, men who lose wives to death more rapidly remarry, often to avoid feeling lost and alone. They will

2   Seb Walker, "Divorce Makes Women Happier than Men," *The Guardian* (July 4, 2005): https://www.theguardian.com/society/2005/jul/04/genderissues.uknews (accessed October 11, 2016).

take this action even when there are numerous red-flag warnings about the new relationship.

Below is a summary chart of some of the basic differences between men and women in their depressive behaviors and how they cope with despair.

Summary of Gender Differences in Expressions of Depression

Men Are More Likely To	Women Are More Likely To
Accuse others, feel angry, and display agitated behavior	Show lots of guilt, feel worthless and overwhelmingly sad, and cry frequently
Hide their depression behind withdrawal or a façade of bluster	Openly express their despair and hopelessness
Feel powerless and a lack of control, with issues of inadequacy	Express feelings of loneliness and anxiety, with issues of insecurity
Trigger conflicts and confrontations, often feeling very defensive and distrusting	Avoid conflicts and confrontations, often placating others excessively
Cope through substance abuse, TV, sports obsessions, or extramarital affairs	Cope by pouring themselves into friends, food, or romantic books and films

Men Are More Likely To	Women Are More Likely To
Live in their own worlds, neglecting spouse and children or viewing them as stressors	Develop dependent relationships with others or center attention on health concerns
Have lots of pessimism and impatience	Have lots of anxiety and confusion
Resist seeking help, seeing it as an admission of weakness	More quickly seek help, hoping for relief from their suffering
Handle loss of a spouse (by divorce or death) by quickly remarrying to quell fear of being alone	Deal with loss of a spouse by using better developed life skills for independent living

Let's face it, men: We're usually not as strong as we think we are—particularly if emotional strength is defined as our ability to adjust to harsh realities. It's time for us to find other, more productive ways to process our sadness and bad feelings. To be fair, women also need guidance to successfully integrate their experiences with that of the men in their lives. Understanding how differently men and women are wired can help bridge the gap between them and how they respond to depression.

Chapter 3

When Men Think Depression Is Unmanly

> The third thing every man should know:
> Most men display a tough exterior
> to cover up their despair.

Jim had recently lost his job due to downsizing. He had worked for his company for twenty years, and this was devastating. Two weeks later, his wife asked for a divorce, citing his heavy drinking and verbally abusive behavior.

For the first time, he thought about suicide, rejecting it (at least for now) to avoid further damaging his children's lives. Nevertheless, he was depressed by his life's profoundly negative turn. He came into counseling only because his mother had urged him to do so.

In counseling, he soon realized that he had been depressed for much longer than recent events would suggest. When everything crashed down on him at once, he had neither the resources nor the emotional stamina to deal with it. Still, he resisted getting help, thinking it would be the true sign of failure. Going to counseling as a favor for his mother, however, was an acceptable reason. For the first time, he allowed himself to talk about the terrible pain he felt inside.

THE PROBLEM OF MISINTERPRETATION

This deeply troubled man demonstrates a pattern that often goes unrecognized as depression. Instead of seeing him as someone struggling to cope with his circumstances, many would interpret his behavior as that of a bully who is finally getting his just desserts. They're likely to think that he just needs to grow up and become more responsible. They may focus on his drinking problem and refer him to AA, or they may worry about his short fuse and refer him to an anger management group. But they often don't recognize the depression for what it is.

When we misinterpret behaviors as something other than depression, we make an unfortunate mistake that will only delay or, perhaps, prevent people from getting timely treatment. This is a common problem. Depressed men are more likely to show symptoms that serve only to aggravate their troubles, not relieve them. These include behaviors like:

- Protracted or explosive anger

- Self-distracting compulsions—drinking, gambling, substance abuse, overspending, etc.

- General irritability and frustration—pushing others away with bad behavior

- Intimidation—showing little tolerance for opposing opinions despite being highly opinionated themselves

- Ill-advised risk-taking—engaging in car or motorcycle racing, acrobatic skydiving, or any number of adrenalin-soaked aggressive activities

- Road rage—yelling and swearing at other drivers and driving erratically

- Creating an emotionally unsafe place—engaging in behaviors such as screaming at or ignoring their children and spouse

- Workaholism—pouring themselves into endless hours of work and neglecting everything else

- Mind-numbing escapism—watching TV, playing computer games, etc.

- Avoidance of God—ditching church, waning in their faith in God, or, perhaps, feeling angry with God for not rescuing them

Some describe depression as rage turned inward against self. However, men may show depression more as anger turned outward—toward spouses, work colleagues, friends, or acquaintances. However, their bluster is only a façade for self-hatred and self-blame. While they may feel hopeless and worthless inside, they hide it—even from themselves. For example, they may indulge in sexual escapades such as affairs, attempting to recapture feelings of importance.

> **Depressed men are more likely to show symptoms that serve only to aggravate their troubles, not relieve them.**

Whatever their avenue of escape, the common theme is a rejection of everything they've valued in the past. When the consequences of their actions finally hit home, they discover that their lives have become even worse than before. Sometimes, it leads to suicidal thoughts.

Because they're often in denial, men don't realize they are actually depressed. They're too busy masking their depressed feelings with other reckless and destructive behaviors. Fueling this denial is the belief that depression is a sign of personal weakness or that depression is primarily a woman's problem.

THE PATH OF LEAST RESISTANCE

Men find it easier to blame physical issues or other people for their difficulties, rather than admit feelings of uselessness and self-hatred. Drinking too much, driving dangerously, or working into the early morning hours may elicit complaints of insensitivity, but they help avoid confronting deeper questions about the despair underneath the behaviors.

While the stoic, tough-it-out attitude may disengage men from their true problems for a while, it can only go so far. Eventually, the sheer weight of negativity drives others (and themselves) to attribute their behavior to something else. Either way, they have lost their bearings, which is why they are likely to question God's purpose in their lives.

With their spiritual lives shutting down, they cannot find solace in the refuge of God's presence as King David did (Psalm 9:9–10). By choice, they slug it out with life on their own. God aches to re-engage his lost children bereft of emotional and spiritual stamina to find their way out. Even in the darkest days of Israel's wanderings in the wilderness of their sin, God proclaimed his desire to bring them back to him (Isaiah 30:18–21).

While women may complain about loneliness, it turns out that men are actually the loneliest people of all. Yes, they may have many acquaintances, but there are few in whom they can find solace during hard times. They rarely take the time to develop the deeply personal relationships that women typically have. Since intimacy is not their thing, they are destined to suffer the absence of empathy from others.

Even when men have so-called buddies, the relationships are normally focused around sports, business, or some such activity. Rarely do they ask penetrating questions, because such questions would be deemed too personal. A man asking another man to share his inner feelings is not considered masculine. Clearly, this consideration does not serve them well when they are depressed and in need of loving counsel.

> **Exploding anger or sullen withdrawal make poor substitutes for honest tears.**

Men believe they must rely only on themselves, that it's somehow weak to submit themselves to the care and counsel of someone else. This idea makes it even harder for them to recognize their depression in the first place. Instead, telling themselves that they're not supposed to be depressed leads to behavior that makes it likely that they'll be misdiagnosed.

Exploding anger or sullen withdrawal make poor substitutes for honest tears—even if experience has taught them that crying is not an option. Rather than face the unpleasant reality of a broken spirit, it is easy for men to disguise depression with more psychologically tolerable habits (such as drug or alcohol abuse) or physical complaints (such as aches and pains or digestive difficulties).

They're not feigning addiction or exhibiting hypochondriasis; they're truly in distress, even if they don't know what the real problem is. They may not call their experience depression, but they still understand that something's wrong. Certainly, they want the pain to go away. Unfortunately, the way they go about it just makes it that much harder for them to overcome the obstacles to seeking the help they need.

PART 2:

THE SURPRISES OF DEPRESSION

Chapter 4

When Depression Accompanies Medical Conditions

> The fourth thing every man should know: Traumatic injury, chronic disease, or disabling disease can have a profoundly negative emotional impact on men.

John, aged fifty-six, suffered a heart attack eight months before he entered counseling with his distressed wife, Margaret. The heart attack was fairly severe, leaving him weakened and subject to bouts of labored breathing if he exerted himself. His wife felt he was distancing himself, showing far less affection and attention than in the past.

She feared that he didn't love her anymore and that he would leave her. She could not figure out how she had alienated him. John insisted that he didn't feel differently and said that they were just getting older and that her expectations of a hot and heavy romance were not realistic. He told her to just give it a rest; he wasn't going anywhere.

It became clear that John was emotionally devastated by the limitations his heart condition had put on him. He had always been very active, often playing basketball at the local gym. Now he felt trapped in a new, invalid body. He secretly pined for his youth when he could do anything he wanted. In short, he was very depressed. Unfortunately, Margaret misinterpreted his lethargy and general disinterest as disaffection with her, causing her to fear their thirty-year marriage was falling apart.

Once she understood what was happening, she was both relieved and determined to stand by him and help. When his depression began to lift, their relationship began to improve. John discovered that his physical limitations brought new ways of leading an active, purposeful life. With the emotional barriers removed, he found, too, that his strength wasn't as limited after all—something his cardiologist had been repeatedly telling him.

Many people, including family members, are unaware that some of the symptoms experienced during a defined illness are really the result of depression. We know, of course, that it's quite common for those suffering from a chronic medical condition to also be clinically depressed. Since depression can easily be concealed under the more prominent symptoms of a person's disease, the patient's emotional state may go undetected and untreated. This is especially true for men, who tend to be less open to their emotional lives.

Due in part to men's more physically oriented view, chronic illnesses or severe injuries can have a huge impact on a man's mental wellbeing. Both the professional athlete and the average guy playing pick-up basketball at the gym can be devastated by a disabling injury or a disease that limits mobility.

Depression can emerge either from the long-term stress of coping with disease or from the limiting consequences of an illness. Knowing this in advance can better prepare them (and family members) to get appropriate help for their mental health should an injury, accident, or debilitating disease strike.

Studies estimate that up to one-third of all chronically ill patients are also depressed. As stated above, this is the result of three things:

1. Restrictions imposed upon them by the disease

2. Decline in quality of life, including the inability to do the activities they once enjoyed

3. Loss of optimism for the future

At least in part, the severity of the illness often determines the severity of the depression.

Ironically, the depression itself can have a negative impact on the very course the medical condition may take. For example, depression can significantly complicate the risks for, and accelerate the consequences of, say, coronary heart disease. When they realize the limits of what they can do have changed, men often sink into despair. They mourn the loss of their physical freedom—and their youth.

For perhaps the first time, they have to worry about their health, which may mean watching more carefully what they eat and making certain that they take their medications. The carefree life, as they see it, has vanished and with it the freedom to do whatever they want. Gone, too, is their sense of invulnerability. It's not hard to understand why they may become depressed.

What they usually don't see is that their depression brings a new level of fatigue of its own. This is why the mind-body issue complicates the healing process. It's helpful to remember that emotional states can affect biological conditions just as much as biological conditions can influence emotional states.

It's important to understand, too, that depression itself is more complex than merely a "chemical imbalance in the brain," as popularly believed. There are many psychological and environmental causal factors as well. So we need to correct our perspective—or we will likely make our physical state grow worse. (See the sidebar "Tips for Correcting Your Perspective.")

Tips for Correcting Your Perspective

The following table gives four primary types of questions you should be asking yourself as well as sample questions.[3]

Type of Question	Sample Questions
Testing Reality	• What evidence is there both for and against my thinking? • Are my thoughts based on facts or just my interpretations? • Am I automatically looking for the negative?
Looking for Other Explanations	• Is there a different way to view this situation? • What other meanings might exist? • What would be a positive perspective on this situation?
Putting Things into Perspective	• Are things as bad as I'm making them out to be? • What's the worst thing that could happen? What's the best thing?

---

3   Ben Martin, PsyD, "Challenging Negative Self-Talk," *PsychCentral* (May 17, 2016): http://psychcentral.com/lib/challenging-negative-self-talk/ (accessed October 11, 2016).

Type of Question	Sample Questions
Putting Things into Perspective *(cont.)*	• How likely is either the best- or worst-case scenario? Which is more likely to happen? • What is good about this situation? • Will this situation even matter to me in five years' time? Will it matter to anyone else?
Using Goal-Oriented Thinking	• Is this way of thinking helping me to feel happy/get well/achieve my goals? • What steps can I take to help me resolve the situation? • What can I learn from this situation that will help me deal with it better next time?

We must intentionally look for the opportunities afforded us by the need to change our lifestyles. The alarm system of depression was never intended to be an unheeded warning that lasts indefinitely. Rather, it's designed to direct our attention to what is problematic in our lives and to resolve it in new and creative ways.

Among the more significant psychological restrictions imposed by disease and/or injury is the possibility of greater isolation. Such isolation can increase feelings of loneliness and hopelessness, which are at the heart of depression.

Without alternative strategies to try or a plan to change, suicidal thoughts may result. For this reason alone, pay attention to the depressive side effects of physical trauma.

MEDICAL FACTORS IN DEPRESSION

The following are the depression rates associated with various chronic medical conditions:[4]

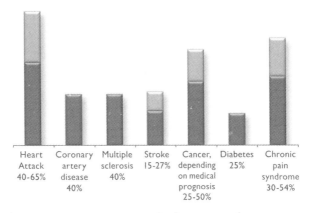

| Heart Attack 40-65% | Coronary artery disease 40% | Multiple sclerosis 40% | Stroke 15-27% | Cancer, depending on medical prognosis 25-50% | Diabetes 25% | Chronic pain syndrome 30-54% |

As you can see, common medical events can have a profound emotional impact on a person's sense of wellbeing. These statistics apply to men and women equally. People are reasonably good at getting the medical attention they need during the height of the crisis.

4   Chronic Illness and Depression," *Cleveland Clinic.* http://
    my.clevelandclinic.org/health/articles/chronic-illness-depression
    (accessed January 12, 2017).

Rarely, however, do they pay much attention to the need for counseling to better cope with the new limitations associated with their disease.

Often, a vicious cycle begins: They have difficulty accepting the frustrating restrictions of their medical condition and become depressed; this, in turn, renders their medical treatment less effective than it could be, which, then, results in even greater depression, and so on.

Several years ago, a happily married pastor in his early sixties became mysteriously depressed. In fact, he became so depressed that he could hardly get out of bed in the morning and carry on with his normal duties. Confused about what was happening, he paid a visit to his family doctor. There he learned, to his surprise, that he had extremely low testosterone levels. He was suffering from male menopause. With the appropriate hormone treatment, his depression lifted and he resumed his duties as pastor with renewed vigor.

You might be thinking menopause is strictly a women's issue. But men also may struggle with it. It often shows up in a man's low energy levels, feelings of physical weakness, dreary mood, and little interest in sex. While depression is the presenting issue, low testosterone is the problem.

Incidentally, there is another medical condition that can result in this problem: *hyperprolactinemia*. This is a condition in which the pituitary gland produces too much of the hormone prolactin, which greatly reduces the production of testosterone. An undetected prolactin-induced decrease in testosterone not only can produce depression but also can reduce the body's ability to absorb calcium, over time causing osteoporosis.

As part of a comprehensive diagnostic evaluation for depression, it's important to get a physical exam. When certain symptoms are present, a good primary-care physician will understand the emotional side effects of a medical condition. And he or she will know to ask questions and/or administer a brief depression scale (like the Hamilton Survey for Emotional and Physical Wellness; see sidebar) to determine the patient's psychological functioning. If your doctor discovers depression is the issue, he or she will usually prescribe antidepressant medication, recommend professional counseling, or both.

The Hamilton Survey for Emotional and Physical Wellness (Ham-D) and the Beck Depression Inventory are brief self-report inventories you can take to get some quick feedback about whether or not you are depressed and, if depressed, how urgent it is to get the help you need. You can find the Hamilton Survey online on the Depression Outreach website (www.Depressionoutreach.com). It includes a self-scoring procedure.

Changes to Your Brain

In recent years, a brain protein known as BDNF (brain-derived neurotrophic factor) has been discovered to play an important role in supporting existing nerve cells and stimulating the growth of new cells in the central nervous system. This protein is most active in areas of the brain vital to learning, memory, and higher thinking.

Physical exercise, psychotherapy, and antidepressant medication have all been shown to increase BDNF synthesis. Chronic, untreated depression, on the other hand, has been found to have the opposite effect: a decrease in BDNF production. What this means is that depression left untreated can lead to deterioration or damage to the brain in the areas responsible for thinking and learning. Keep in mind that should you forego help, this effect could have a significant impact on the quality of your later mental life.

Making the Most of What You Have

If you're depressed due to a chronic medical condition, push yourself to stay actively engaged with life. It's very easy to isolate yourself, but it's important to resist that temptation. Otherwise, the resulting emotional downward spiral could lead to further deterioration of your chronic condition and increase the physical limitations you already have.

As believers, we know that God can use our circumstances to teach us something new (either about ourselves or about him) or to further his kingdom in some unexpected way. A woman who lived in late nineteenth-century England and who attended a church that had fallen on hard times spiritually experienced this. She was determined to work toward a revival of her church's zeal for serving God. But a short time later, she was afflicted with a disease that left her bedridden for the rest of her life. Unable to attend church, she lapsed into severe depression.

> **God never lets a situation go to waste, if we have the faith to see it through on his terms, not ours.**

One day a friend suggested that she could faithfully pray for the spiritual renewal of her church. She decided that this was what God wanted from her. Year after year, she prayed every day, for much of the day, for her church to experience spiritual renewal. After hearing about the work of Dwight L. Moody in America, she began to pray that Moody might preach at her church.

After nearly ten years of praying, Dwight L. Moody came to England to learn from other pastors and preachers. There he met the pastor of the woman's church, Reverend John Lessey, who asked Moody if he might preach at the church. Moody agreed, intending to preach that one Sunday and then move on to Ireland.

But the response from that little church was so overwhelming, he was called back from Ireland to continue the revival that had begun. He ended up staying for ten days, during which time hundreds came to know Christ. He later returned to England for an extended campaign, which lasted for two years. In London alone, a quarter of a million people were able to attend Moody's meetings.

When this woman heard what had happened, she realized that God had honored her faithful service for all of those years. God had used her in a mighty way, even though she was severely limited by her medical condition.

I said earlier that God never lets a situation go to waste, if we have the faith to see it through on his terms, not ours. James 5:17–18 tells us:

> "Elijah was a human being, even as we are. He prayed earnestly that it would not rain, and it did not rain on the land for three and a half years. Again he prayed, and the heavens gave rain, and the earth produced its crops."

We might ask in astonishment, "Elijah was like us?" When was the last time you prayed and something like a dramatic change in the weather pattern happened? What could James possibly mean by such an outlandish statement?

James is saying that while Elijah prayed for big things with a heart of conviction, we tend to ask for small things with a faint heart. If we will take him at his word, God can dispel our depression with meaning and purpose, even when we may be limited by a disabling medical condition. It may not be the outcome we expect, but—still better— it's one that God himself ordains.

The consistent prayers of that obscure but faithful woman living in a rural area of England succeeded in changing, not just her depression and the spiritual condition of her church, but also the spiritual condition of her nation and the life of Dwight Moody who has influenced countless lives throughout the world! Who'd have thought a physically shrunken, bedridden woman in a small insignificant English church could have had that kind of impact? She mattered more than anyone could imagine. That's because she first mattered to God.

Chapter 5

Prescriptions as Two-Edged Swords

> **The fifth thing every man should know: Some prescription drugs can have distinctly depressive side effects.**

Sometimes, even after careful consideration, the cause of your depression remains a mystery. Perhaps that's when it's time to look at the medications you are currently taking. Many times, depression is either a side effect of taking medications or the result of withdrawing from medications.

EXPLAINING THE UNEXPLAINED

At times, depression seems to come from out of the blue. This could mean the depression was triggered by something biological in origin. For example, bipolar disorder (with its manic and depressive phases) requires a combination of medications. Occasionally this disorder is misdiagnosed as simply depression alone, and an antidepressant is prescribed. However, in this case, antidepressants given alone increase the likelihood of a manic episode, something to avoid. It's important, then, to get the correct diagnosis before beginning medication.

Medications Associated with Depression

Check out any medications you recently started taking. Below is a brief list of medications that can have depression as a side effect.

Blood Pressure Medications (antihypertensives)

- Beta blockers (Inderal)
- Calcium channel blockers (Diltiazem, Cardizem)
- Nifedipine (Procardia)

- Methyldopa (Aldomet)
- Guanethidine sulfate (Ismelin sulfate)
- Clonidine hydrochloride (Catapres)

Anti-Parkinson's Disease Agents

- Carbidopa-levodopa (Sinemet)
- Amantadine hydrochloride (Dopar, Larodopa, Symmetrel)

Anti-Anxiety Agents: Benzodiazepines (especially withdrawal after addiction)

- Diazepam (Valium)
- Chlordiazepoxide (Librium)
- Xanax
- Clonazepam (Klonopin)
- Flurazepam (Dalmane)
- Lorazepam (Ativan)
- Triazolam (Halcion)

Psychoactive Substances

- Alcohol
- Opiates (opium, heroin, codeine, Hydrocodone, Methadone, Morphine, Darvocet, Oxycodone [Oxycontin], Percocet, Percodan, Vicodin, Meperidine [Demerol])

- Amphetamines
- Cocaine
- Anabolic steroids

Barbiturates

- Phenobarbital
- Secobarbital

Anticonvulsants

- Ethosuximide (Zarontin)
- Methsuximide (Celontin)

Statins (used to reduce cholesterol)

- Atorvastatin (Lipitor)
- Fluvastatin (Lescol)
- Pravastatin (Pravachol)
- Simvastatin (Zocor)

Chemotherapy Agents

- Vincristine, Vinblastine, Procarbazine, Interferon

First Generation Antipsychotic Medications

- Phenothiazines (Thorazine, Mellaril, Stelazine, Trilafon, Phenergan)
- Haloperidol (Haldol)

Acne Medications

- Isotretinoin (Accutane, Sotret)

Anti-Smoking Medication

- Varenicline (Chantix)

Medication to Herpes and Shingles

- Acyclovir (Zovirax)

WITHDRAWING FROM MEDICATIONS

Because of emotional side effects, withdrawing from some drugs—particularly benzodiazepines and opiates—requires the utmost caution. Make sure you withdraw from these agents only under a doctor's supervision. Sudden withdrawal from these drugs, especially if you have been taking them regularly for a long time or at a high dosage level, can have severe, even dangerous, side effects—including acute depression. Many people are unaware of this and simply decide to go off of them on their own. This is very unwise—with any medication.

If you're taking one of the medications listed above, talk to your doctor if you're suffering from the blues. If you are taking a medication not on the list above, still talk with your doctor about whether or not your medication could be responsible for your negative mood.

You may be fearful of many of the things connected with your illness:

- What lies ahead in the course of your disease

- Your changing physical appearance

- Whether your illness is likely to lead to greater incapacitation

- Your medications' possible side effects

Consequently, it's wise to seek professional counsel to guide you through this difficult time.

"Therefore we do not lose heart.... For our light
and momentary troubles are achieving for us an
eternal glory that far outweighs them all."
—2 Corinthians 4:16–17

FREELANCING WITH YOUR PHYSICAL AND MENTAL HEALTH

Abusing drugs to cope with your emotional pain can cost a lot to your health and worsen your depression during withdrawal from them. The opiates men tend to consume cover a wide range—morphine, codeine, Hydrocodone, Oxycodone, Percocet, Percodan, and Vicodin. Most of these drugs are used by physicians to treat acute and chronic pain. But many are abused by drug-addicted patients using the medication to numb their emotional pain. What makes opiates so addictive is that they produce a false sense of wellbeing, or euphoria, along with their pain-relieving properties.

Overuse of these drugs is by no means a harmless pleasure. Tolerance to their euphoric effects (which means a person must take more and more of it to experience the same sense of wellbeing, or euphoria) develops faster than their physical tolerance to the drugs' potentially lethal effects (such as cardiac or respiratory arrest [hypoxia]). And rapid withdrawal can produce fatigue, agitation, anxiety, insomnia, and a lack of motivation—all of which can aggravate a prior depressive state.

Much the same can be said for recreational drugs, such as methamphetamine, cocaine, and anabolic steroids.

One difference is that use of these drugs can have an immediate, dire—even fatal—impact on your body. They can also have a devastating emotional impact, including acute depression. When these drugs are used and abused, your depression has become an excuse to take you to the edge of complete self-destruction.

Two-Edged Swords

Prescription drugs, as well as street drugs, are usually two-edged swords, capable of different physical and emotional effects, both positive and negative. In their medical uses, there is a certain tradeoff between their healing and damaging properties, which the doctor must consider when prescribing them. When it comes to recreational drugs, there is often an indifference to their dangerous properties, largely because there are self-destructive thoughts or behaviors underlying the drug abuse in the first place.

The goal of investigating medications is to develop the ability to ask the right questions when considering all the risk factors that might contribute to your emotional state at any given point in time. Only when you are in possession of the facts are you in a position to make wise decisions. And remember, the older you are, the greater your risk.

ABUSING DRUGS

The unique characteristics of male depression leave men susceptible to abuse medications or to use drugs illegally to handle emotional distress. While a sense of worthlessness leads women to blame themselves, men tend to blame others, stoking their anger and irritability, as well as their sense of victimhood. Although women are more likely to feel anxious and lonely, avoiding conflicts whenever they can, men are more often distrusting, apprehensive, and agitated, resulting in a higher chance of conflict. Women more readily admit to feeling hurt, while men admit little and, instead, seek solace in self-medication (drugs, alcohol, sex, sports, etc.).

In short, men's dealing with life's setbacks and disappointments is more acting out than problem solving. Problem solving suggests change, which means to them that what they've been doing is wrong or unhelpful. This strikes at the heart of their feelings of inadequacy—a major reason for their anger and defensiveness. The destructive self-victimization that follows merely deepens their depression and intensifies their attempts to self-medicate.

A QUESTION OF SERVICE

Scripture tells us that from the beginning, man (Adam) was endowed with all the attributes necessary to maintain harmony in God's created order. But when Adam and Eve decided that wasn't enough, they lost their way. Ever since the fall, man has been vulnerable to an underlying concern with power and control, and depression in men typically results from feelings of helplessness and impotence.

God has no desire for us to languish—spiritually or emotionally—in an endless quest for control. When the disciples argued over who would be the greatest in heaven, Jesus gently guided them into an understanding of greatness in the eyes of God, and they finally came to realize that it's humble service to others that attracts God's attention (Matthew 18:1–4; 20:24–28). Such service means letting go of power and control. Obviously, this wasn't easy for these men to accept.

It may be difficult for us as well, but we would do well to likewise let go of our quest for power and control and embrace service to others. Contact your church office to find out about ways you can serve the members of your church and community.

PART 3:

IDEAS AND BEHAVIORS
THAT HURT

Chapter 6

Exposing the Spiritual Stereotypes

> **The sixth thing every man should know:
> What you believe about who God is
> and how he relates to us can be a
> factor of depression.**

A profoundly depressed man sought out several members of his Bible study for help. Each was convinced that his depression demonstrated a lack of faith in God. They prayed over him, anointed him with oil, and offered up intercessory prayer for him. He pleaded with God to rebuild his faith and lift him out of his despair. He did everything that was asked of him, but his depression remained.

When he came to see me, he was questioning his salvation. In fact, he was becoming angry at God for leaving him, though he dared not share that with his friends.

During the course of counseling, we discussed several important factors contributing to his depression. We looked at the story of Job from the Bible. We looked at how Job's friends tried to help but to no avail. We looked at Job's anger at God, his deep disillusionment with life, and, most importantly, how God did not save the day right away. God had momentous things to teach Job, but he needed Job's full attention, which his depression served to provide.

Job finally understood in much greater depth the One whom he worshipped. He was a changed man, who, at last, found peace. We read that "the LORD blessed the latter part of Job's life more than the former part" (Job 42:12).

In James 1:4, James suggests it's perhaps better to pray, not to be rescued, but rather for perseverance to endure (Greek word, *hupomenen*, meaning "to remain under") circumstances until God has completed his work in us. That's not something we would come to on our own, since everything inside us screams out for immediate relief.

"Let perseverance finish its work so that you may be mature and complete, not lacking anything."
—James 1:4

When this depressed man heard these words, he realized that God was using his depression in much the same way as he did with Job. God was teaching him about unresolved issues that were affecting his relationships in negative ways—including his relationship with God. What was left of his depression lifted as he relished his new understanding. Along the way, his faith was refreshed.

His friends were well-intentioned but didn't understand his depression. The church is comprised of imperfect people striving in very imperfect ways to support each other. Often, hurting believers try to help other hurting believers without really understanding what God is doing. As a result, false stereotypes of depression can flourish in the church.

FOUR STEREOTYPES OF DEPRESSION

Stereotypes of depression are harmful to those struggling with depression. They create spiritual self-doubts and fears of failing God that only make things worse. Four such stereotypes are of particular note.

Stereotype #1: Depression as Sin

The idea that it's sinful to be depressed springs from the false notion that our faith is a ticket to a happy life. As a result, it is believed that emotional crises are indications that the person needs rebuke.

Depression itself can never be a sin, even though it can be the *result* of sin. Depression is an emotional state that serves as an alarm signal warning us that something is wrong. As signals, emotional states are always morally neutral. Remember also that emotions are part of the divine image in man and, as such, reflect our Creator.

The apostle Paul said it best when he remarked, "In your anger do not sin" (Ephesians 4:26). In other words, being angry (the emotional state) is not a sin, but what you do with it can be. He then went on to describe the problems of acted-out rage, bitterness, and revenge, which are indeed sins.

Depression itself is not a sin, but the damaging things we might do while we are depressed can be. Personal responsibility comes from what we plan and do, not from our depressive state of mind when we do it.

Stereotype #2: Depression as a Lack of Faith

This stereotype says that depression reflects a spiritual failure, a deficient trust in God's promises. This minimizes or ignores the role of painful circumstances as a consequence of living in a fallen world. In the Old

Testament, we read about the following men who suffered from depression:

Name	Scripture Reference	Description
Samuel	1 Samuel 8:4–9	The prophet Samuel emotionally fell apart, feeling rejected, because the people demanded a warrior king "such as all the other nations have." God did not rebuke Samuel but comforted him instead.
Elijah	1 Kings 19:1–5; 11–18	Elijah became depressed when the people failed to repent in response to his victory over the prophets of Baal. God told him that the Israelites' stubbornness was not his fault.
Jonah	Jonah 3–4	Jonah became angry and depressed when his mortal enemies repented and God withheld his judgment on them. God responded by encouraging Jonah to change his perspective.
Moses	Exodus 18:13–23; Numbers 11:1–24	Moses became depressed because he could never seem to please the people he served. He even accused God of punishing him with the burden of taking care of his people. Yet God gently redirected him to delegate authority so that he wouldn't burn out in his ministry.

There are many other examples of depression in the Bible—none having anything to do with a lack of faith. Yet many still believe depression is due to just that. They pour on the guilt trips for depressed Christians to read the Bible more and pray that God would give them faith. As a result, depressed Christians become even more depressed when their efforts to be more faithful fail to lift their persistent despair.

Stereotype #3: Depression as God's Punishment

This view paints God as a dictator waiting to pounce on you for every miscue or sinful lapse. From this perspective, God is someone to fear, not one in whom you might find comfort and compassion. He becomes the avenger, not the Good Shepherd.

Remember, fearing God in the biblical sense means viewing him with awe, having great reverence. It reflects a healthy relationship with your heavenly Father, one that's subject to his open heart, not fearfully dreading a closed fist of condemnation.

Believers who struggle with a lot of self-hatred are quite prepared to see depression as an expression of God's justice, not as an occasion for his tender guidance. A man who thinks this way regularly beat himself with a hammer. The client who did this explained, "I'm comfortable to be condemned; that's why I beat myself as a child. God wants me to be guilty and condemned. I'm safer from God if I punish myself first. It's terrifying to be guilty all the time." This client's mother had constantly berated him throughout his childhood, telling him he was destined for hell where God would punish him forever.

Righteousness without forgiveness, and vengeance without mercy are what people like this man really expect—not God's grace. This stereotype ignores the words of the prophet Jeremiah (who battled despair in his own life): "'I know the plans I have for you,' declares the Lord, 'plans to prosper you *and not to harm you, plans to give you hope and a future'*" (Jeremiah 29:11, emphasis added). These words of promise are not just for Jeremiah but for all of God's children.

Stereotype #4: Depression as Demon Possession

This view assumes that depression is evidence of the work of demons and can only be addressed by some sort of exorcism. This act, or ritual, is either done by someone trained in the rituals of exorcism or by concerned fellow believers who, in the name of God, will collectively pray for and anoint the afflicted person.

However, even the New Testament makes a distinction between the demon possessed and those suffering from psychological disorders. In Matthew 4:24 (*KJV*), for example, we read about the people brought to Jesus for healing. These people "were taken with divers diseases and torments" [were physically sick], those who "were possessed with devils," and those who "were lunatick" [Greek for "moonstruck"]. The term *lunatic* originated from Latin and was commonly used to refer to people struggling with a disorder of the mind.

Scripture distinguishes as separate groups those suffering from demon possession and those dealing with mental disorders. Therefore we should do the same. While depression might accompany cases of demon possession, it does *not* follow that depression is itself an expression of demon possession. The very thought that they are demon possessed often drives depressed believers to the brink of desperation. This is especially true if, after submitting to exorcism rituals, their mood fails to improve.

SPIRITUAL BEINGS

If you subscribe to one or another of these stereotypes of depression common among believers, the likelihood is that it has only made things worse. Since we're spiritual as well as psychological beings, feeling hopeless and despondent will affect the quality of our spiritual lives. Dwelling in despair and shame can affect our view of God as one who cares about us. And when that happens, our last shred of optimism vanishes with it.

The truth is that God offers you a second chance at life, a release from the lies you have told yourself. We are defined, not by our sin, nor by our past, but rather by our faith in God's grace and mercy. You are—and always will be—the child of his creation and, therefore, of great worth. Just as you made a decision to embrace Christ as your Savior, you can embrace the comfort of your inestimable worth to him. That means meditating on his words to let the message sink into your heart, not just into your head.

It also means asking yourself how you would *act* differently if you truly believed the message and then acting that way despite your doubts. Sometimes, you can act your way into a new way of thinking more quickly than you can think your way into a new way of acting.

Chapter 7

Seeking Help or Saving Face?

> The seventh thing every man should know: Fear of self-disclosure prevents men from connecting meaningfully with others and from seeking help.

Robert, aged twenty-eight, sat alone in his apartment, staring into his half-empty glass of beer, thinking that he'd had enough of drugs and one-night stands. "What's the point of living?" he asked himself. "Everyone lets you down anyway, even my boss. I thought I could count on him, but he let me go! Nothing makes sense anymore. I just want out."

He finished his drink, picked up a loaded gun, and put it to his head. At that moment, his Christian friend Dave knocked at his door, asking Robert to go to church with him. Robert agreed. He thought, "It's one last favor for a friend on my way out of the world."

In the church foyer after the service, Robert grabbed his surprised friend and fell to his knees. Sobbing, he made one last desperate plea to God for mercy and compassion—for some kind of purpose in life. Others quickly surrounded him, kneeling and placing hands on his trembling shoulders, praying for God to meet him in his hour of despair. That night, Robert accepted Christ as his Savior. At last, he was free of his burden of meaninglessness.

> **In this country alone, roughly six million men suffer from depression.**

Shortly after that, he had the wisdom (as he said, "from God") to seek counseling to deal with some of the issues that had prompted him to self-medicate with drugs and sex. As counseling progressed, he grew, not only in his faith, but in his overall emotional health as well.

Robert's story had a wonderful ending. However, others do not. There is an alarming worldwide trend of a sharp increase in the suicide rate of younger men. In this country alone, roughly six million men suffer from depression, and those are only the ones who have actually reported it. However, since men generally don't recognize their symptoms and resist getting help even if they do, it's hard to know the real numbers.

We have mentioned the risk factors for men, which include

- Divorce
- Death
- Unemployment
- Retirement
- Drugs and alcohol
- Chronic illness
- Lack of meaningful friendships

We can add to these factors the problem of being in any occupation, like medicine (especially psychiatry), that bears responsibility for the welfare of others and has convenient access to the means of suicide.

Men tend to prefer being alone over self-disclosure. *Self-disclosure* is the process of revealing your thoughts—emotions, fears, dreams, failures, successes, etc.—to someone else. Men dislike self-disclosure because it leaves them feeling vulnerable. They will do anything to avoid looking foolish or overreactive to others. Baring their souls is hardly an attractive alternative to stoically holding it all in.

Ironically, you are already communicating your feelings through nonverbal behavior. Everyone around you is going to know that something is wrong if you

- Have a short fuse,
- Become more frequently intoxicated,

- Start slamming doors and kicking holes in the wall, and/or
- Radically withdraw from social interaction.

You may not use words, but you're still clearly broadcasting your depression.

In reality, talking about it with someone who cares and is trained to help you is far more likely to be useful. Sadly, the great majority of men struggling with depression never seek help of any kind. In fact, 90 percent or more of African-American males do not seek such treatment.

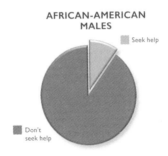

AFRICAN-AMERICAN MALES

Seek help

Don't seek help

PRIORITIES THAT HAVE BEEN MISPLACED

Men's fear of appearing weak is often greater than their desire to do something about their pain. Unfortunately, in their marriages, their denial comes across as indifference to their spouses' needs. I have had many wives tell me that they feel unloved by their depressed husbands. But if they directly tell their husbands (and some do), the husband's depression only deepens—chalking up one more failure.

When men first come in to see me—particularly if they are with their wives—they are guarded, scoping out the situation, often expecting to be judged. They need reassurance that they are not going to be held solely to blame for their predicament. Only then do they settle down to the task of therapy and begin to open up. The adequacy issue, you see, is almost always there, residing just underneath the surface.

FOUR BARRIERS TO RECOGNIZING DEPRESSION

You might think that since depressed people are sad and hopeless, it would be easy to spot in yourself and others. But with the often-confusing overlap of other conditions, it's not as easy as it sounds. Several barriers to recognizing depression can exist.

Barrier #1: The Question of Physical Complications

Depression shares a number of symptoms with physical disease:

- Fatigue
- Loss of appetite
- Loss of sexual interest
- Difficulty sleeping
- Aches and pains

Symptoms like these can suggest that the men have a low-grade virus. Their discouragement and anxiety are ascribed to a physical illness—something they fear is hanging on and could be serious. Such depressed people may choose to seek medical advice, but more often, they decide to wait it out, hoping that it will clear up on its own. If their discomfort continues indefinitely, they may finally go to their doctor and be surprised to learn that they are not physically ill but depressed.

Even then, they may very well decide to forego psychological services, thinking that since there is no medical issue involved, there is no immediate need to take action. Of course, it's their fears that are doing the talking here, not the voice of reason. Nonetheless, it gives them relief to think of seeing a therapist as a last resort.

Barrier #2: Presuming a Character Weakness

When someone believes that depression shows weakness in character, it is even harder to recognize depression for what it is. When you feel threatened by the idea that you could be depressed or experiencing any emotional disorder, you're more likely to slip into denial. You simply don't want to acknowledge to yourself that you're unable to cope.

Usually, the response is to create a tough-guy façade of someone who doesn't need any help but instead blames everyone or everything else for his troubles. Essentially, you're left with two options:

1. Try to hang in there, hoping things will turn around on their own.

2. Admit defeat and completely withdraw.

Both options will likely push treatment away from your door. Remember, transparency—first with yourself and then with others—is key to breaking out of that trap.

It takes strength to admit to depression, face the issues, stop putting yourself down as weak, and regain your foothold on mental health. It may take counseling to properly sort out all the issues, but that step, too, takes courage. Have the courage to pursue genuine emotional growth.

Barrier #3: Over-Spiritualizing the Problem

When you subscribe to spiritual stereotypes (see chapter 6), you are almost certain to view emotional struggles as spiritual deficiency. But remember that the emotional state itself is always morally neutral. If you fail to understand this, you'll end up shooting the messenger (depression) because you reject the message alerting you to the problem(s) you've ignored—or at least endured—up until now.

In case you think this minimizes the spiritual component in emotional struggles, the problem depression is pointing to could very well involve spiritual issues. Like Job whose spiritual walk wasn't the problem, God may want to enlarge your concept of who he is and what he can really do in your life. Before that concept can change, however, you may need to deal with unresolved emotional issues first.

When you feel ashamed of depression, falsely thinking it reveals spiritual deficiency, you're probably going to hide your misery from other believers. Unfortunately, doing so cuts you off from getting the very support you need in your efforts to heal. Even worse, you also deny yourself the counseling that could help you.

Barrier #4: The Financial Cost of Counseling

Surveys show that worries about the cost of counseling have inhibited the pursuit of treatment, especially among men. As one depressed pastor said, "The Scriptures are my therapist, and they don't charge me 100 dollars per hour." Of course, when his emotional pain became so excruciating that he was seriously considering suicide, he sought professional help. Once in treatment and experiencing its value, his tune changed.

While cost can sometimes be a factor, men will use this as a rationale to avoid treatment. Since many insurance plans now cover psychological counseling services, and some treatment plans are available on a prorated basis according to the ability to pay, this reasoning loses its weight. Some of the same people citing cost as prohibitive to care are at the same time buying iPhones, iPads, flat-screen high-definition televisions, new cars, etc. They are unwittingly telling themselves that they are not worth the cost, even though their material possessions are. Remember, it's how you *treat* yourself that determines how you really think of yourself.

MARITAL TUG-OF-WAR

Another reason men avoid treatment is because they don't want to give in to their wives' demands to get counseling. This is a power game and a lose-lose battle, since the loser's bitterness inevitably destroys the winner's victory. Win-win positions are much more likely to have happier outcomes. What's more, they lead to a shared journey through the husband's depression—a key to success in treatment.

Sometimes, when a wife presents her husband with the ultimatum of treatment or a divorce, the man may grudgingly attend counseling sessions but sabotage the session by passively declining participation in any sort of change—he is there in body but not in spirit.

No real good can come from this tactic. That's why power games in a relationship rarely achieve their objective. These divisive maneuvers only guarantee that a partner's depression will spread to the marriage and doom it to mutually assured destruction.

DEPRESSION AND THE SECULAR CULTURE

According to one study, the number of people diagnosed with depression steadily increases every year at roughly a 20-percent rate of growth. It is hard to say whether this is due to more rigorous diagnostic procedures, greater public awareness, or simply a higher incidence of depression. But we do know that this increase correlates with the growing sense of meaninglessness and lack of purpose that typically accompanies the rise of a secular, materialistic culture.

In a secular, materialistic culture, man's spirituality is dismissed as unimportant, shriveling the divine image. Our understanding of the reason for our existence slowly disappears. And with it, so does our sense of stability and optimism.

If depression dominates your life, consider how much others define your reality. Considering it *unmanly* to accept help or to discuss how you feel reveals the cultural stereotypes in your thinking. God calls us to courageously try alternatives that represent our willingness as men to step out of our comfort zones.

The Bible tells us that when the disciples asked Jesus how to pray, he said, among other things, that they were not merely to make requests of God but also

- to seek solutions (look for different options) and
- to knock on doors (actually experiment with those options).

The God of the universe invited them into partnership with him—an assertive partnership that called for their active participation. Is that not astonishing? They—and we—are God's sons, nurtured by a loving Father. This point, which never ceases to amaze, was the point of the parable about the prodigal son (Luke 15:11–32).

"Ask and it will be given to you; seek and you will find; knock and the door will be opened to you."
—*Matthew 7:7*

In Matthew 7:7, we read the promise that the Father will open doors that lead to our best interests but that we must first turn the doorknobs. Reaching out to others, like reaching out to God, means travelling on the road of strengthening relationship bonds. This is a road little used by men but one that requires a level of assertiveness that couldn't be more masculine.

Compare the differences between the passivity of withdrawal, aggression toward others, and assertiveness:

Passivity of withdrawal	Reveals disrespect for yourself	You retreat.	You show weakness.
Aggression	Demonstrates disrespect for others	You rebel.	You show defensiveness.
Assertiveness	Reveals respect for both self and others	You serve.	You show confidence and humility.

Respect and confidence are the cornerstones of courage and the basis for open, direct, and appropriate communication. When you are assertive, instead of *wanting* things to happen, you make things happen.

> **Respect and confidence are the cornerstones of courage.**

For many depressed men, this may seem overwhelming at first. Trusting relationships don't happen quickly or spontaneously. Nonetheless they are an important step toward healing the wounds that paralyze you and reduce your world to a dark and sinister place.

PART 4:

THE THERAPY AND THEOLOGY OF HOPE

Chapter 8

Changing the Narrative about Change

> **The eighth thing every man should know: It takes courage to tackle personal growth and question your preconceptions.**

As our sessions came to an end, Shawn said, "This whole process was so much better than I thought it would be. I figured if I just checked the boxes, my wife and friends would stop hounding me about counseling. I didn't think it would really do any good. I thought the same thing about medication. But I was wrong on both counts. I just didn't realize how depressed I was or even what it meant. Honestly, I didn't think I could do anything about it. Boy, am I glad none of that's true!"

These were the heartfelt sentiments of a man happy with his transformation. He realized that his misconceptions had long kept him from getting help. He was relieved to discover that his depression had a purpose. And by resolving his longstanding problems, he experienced a freedom he never thought possible.

He knew also that if depression returned, it was telling him something needed his attention. Gone were his expectations of a life out of his control. Instead, he welcomed a proactive lifestyle more solution-focused than problem-centered.

As this client's testimony shows, if you do the work, change is possible. Depression is an alarm signal that turns itself off once problem issues are resolved. It takes patience and endurance, but better days are ahead if you unravel the problems that depression is demanding that you address.

Steps to Making a Difference

This process does not happen overnight, but there are steps you can take:

1. Recognize that your depression is telling you to look at interactions that hurt you in the past and will continue hurting you unless you do something different.

2. Dig into these issues, perhaps with a Christian professional counselor. It takes courage to work through the pain caused by past interactions. But it's the only way to erase the power they've had over you.

3. Develop new strategies of living that are more solution-focused than problem-centered. This means experimenting with the challenging and liberating work of personal change.

Bear these principles in mind as the foundations for healing hearts and minds are explored. Remember that God knows we can become overwhelmed by life's trials and also by examining how they've damaged us. As he did with Job and Moses, he understands our despair and even the heated accusations against him. He knows these reactions come from profound brokenness.

Thankfully, we don't serve an emotionally fragile God who becomes defensive when questioned. Instead, he freely offers us his wisdom—wisdom that provides patience and endurance when we need it most.

How Joy Fits In

In James 1:2, we are told, "Consider it pure joy, my brothers and sisters, whenever you face trials of many kinds."

- What can that possibly mean?

- Are we supposed to be masochists?

- Are we supposed to cheer when our business fails or our job is terminated?

- Are we to celebrate the collapse of our marriages, high-five it when someone sues us, or break out the champagne when our homes are foreclosed?

Of course not!

Having joy in the midst of struggle means we believe that God is at work in our person, crafting something better. But no one would say that you should be happy that you're fighting a battle with depression.

> **Joy is defined by James as an enduring supernatural delight in the purpose of God regardless of the circumstances.**

Happiness is the fleeting emotion of cheerful situations. You're happy, for instance, when your favorite football team wins the game or when your candidate wins the election. However, joy is defined by James as an enduring supernatural delight in the purpose of God regardless of the circumstances.

Finding Joy in the Midst of Sorrow

Corrie ten Boom, a Dutch-born watchmaker and
Christian, was imprisoned by the Nazis for helping Jews
escape the Holocaust. She and her sister, with their
unmitigated optimism in God's goodness, completely
baffled their fellow captives to whom they ministered in
the Nazi death camp at Ravensbrück.

Corrie famously said, "If you look to the world, you'll
be distressed; if you look within, you'll be depressed;
if you look to God, you'll be at rest." In effect, she was
saying that the only way to have peace in such a cruel
environment was to find God's righteousness sufficient.
God's nurture and compassion were all they had left, but
for these two sisters, that was enough.

Staying the Course

James makes a radical proposal to try praying, not to ask
God to change the conditions, but to "let perseverance
finish its work" (James 1:4). In other words, ask God to
give you the emotional strength to stay the course until
he has completed his work in you.

That kind of prayer is, to say the least, counterintuitive.
Few people actually pray that way. Most find their pain
too great to consider anything but a prayer for relief. Yet
here is James suggesting that a certain kind of joy can still
come from pain.

Dealing with Trials and Tribulations

Such a prayer would have been foreign to Job, that Old Testament figure synonymous with trials and tribulations. Because of his appalling circumstances, we are impressed all the more by his patience and perseverance (James 5:11). But what did Job's actions actually look like?

He wished he were dead.	Job 3:1
He talked at length about his hopelessness and victim mindset.	Job 6:11–13
He blamed God for bringing his anxiety and misery upon him.	Job 6:2–4
He agonized over his insomnia.	Job 7:2–6
He spoke of his false guilt.	Job 9:20
He seethed in his anger, accusing God of being pleased to oppress him while smiling on the schemes of the wicked.	Job 10:1–3
He described his increasing paranoia and his torturing loneliness.	Job 19:14,19
He fleshed out his feelings of injustice, crying out, "Why should I not be impatient?"	Job 21:4

When we know Job's true thoughts, we find him less a hero and more like you and me when we have trials. You might be asking what it was that prompted James to write that Job was honored for his perseverance. The answer is found in God's response to Job's complaints as contrasted to his response to Job's friends.

First, we should note that when God responded to Job—contrary to our human tendency to shut down and avoid vulnerability—God actually opened himself up. He presented Job with an expanded view of his majesty and sovereign power. Even before he was physically and materially restored, Job understood this as a special moment in his relationship to God: "Surely I spoke of things I did not understand, things too wonderful for me to know" (Job 42:3).

Then God turned to Eliphaz the Temanite, one of Job's friends, and said, "I am angry with you and your two friends, because you have not spoken the truth about me, *as my servant Job has*" (Job 42:7, emphasis added). Job's emotional response to his plight was similar to what ours would have been. In this key moment, God was honoring Job for his moral and intellectual honesty. In contrast, his friends had been playing legalistic head games with him, presenting a picture of God that was untrue.

The Bible is saying that both an open acknowledgment of our problems and our willingness to entertain a different perspective are necessary for personal change. That means taking a closer look at why our thinking and behavior have departed from reality and then challenging the perceived status quo.

PRECONCEPTIONS TO CHALLENGE

In therapeutic terms, one way we identify the origins of anxiety and depression is through the *ABC Model* of analysis, which we do in preparation for examining the differences in the ways we respond to life events. In shorthand form, it looks like the following:

- **A** = The **A**CTIVATING event, which is any experiential event that eventuates in (not causes) an emotionally significant response

- **B** = The **B**ELIEFS you have about the activating event which trigger the emotionally significant response

- **C** = The emotional response that occurred as a **C**ONSEQUENCE of the particular beliefs about the activating event

Let's say, for example, you went to a final interview for a job you very much wanted, but you failed to be hired. When I meet you later on the street, you are angry, frustrated, and very depressed. If I ask you why you are so depressed, you will probably tell me about the interview and the fact that you lost the job. But then I would respond by saying that that is not the real reason you're depressed. Of course, you would no doubt vigorously protest my response by arguing that losing the job was naturally the reason; obviously, if you had gotten the job, you would have been happy.

Let's examine this exchange:

- Failing to get the job is the activating event (A).

- The emotional consequence (C)—the frustration and depression you experienced—was wrongly assumed by you to be due to A.

- However, C was due to your beliefs (B) about the activating event.

You likely said to yourself that because you didn't get the job, your one chance at the brass ring was lost. As a result, you'll never get the job you want, and you'll be flipping burgers all your life. If you believe that, of course you'll be depressed.

But what if you had said to yourself:

- Losing the job was disappointing, yet I did make it to the final interview, which means I did pretty well.

- There are other good jobs out there, so if I just go after them, I know eventually I'll get one of them.

While you may have been rightly disappointed, instead of spirally down into depression, you would have become even more determined to go back out and look for a job.

You see, what you tell yourself (your beliefs, B) is what underlies the emotional consequence (C)—not the activating event (A), which was the same in either narrative. This is why different people react differently to the same events. It may also be one reason why you're depressed about the setbacks in your life instead of determining to make them better.

The Internal Narrative Dilemma

Often we make bad situations worse by spicing our internal narratives with phrases like:

- *I have to*

- *I must*

- *I can't stand it*

- *It's horrible / awful*

- *I should*

This kind of language greatly (and needlessly) emotionalizes our self-talk. It's called *need language*, because such language is relevant only to true needs being thwarted in some way—blocking something that is necessary for survival. When survival is truly at stake, we usually panic. Rarely are we peaceful. There are very few actual needs in life: food, air, shelter. Most everything else is a preference. To say you don't like what's happening in a given situation (preference language) is far different from saying you can't stand it (need language). It's clearly a lie to tell yourself that you have to have something or be somewhere at a certain time, that it's awful to sit in traffic, or that it's horrible to be inconvenienced by someone. Unpleasant, maybe. Catastrophic, hardly.

The next time you start to get upset about something, ask yourself if your survival is on the line. If it isn't (which is almost always the case), then ask why you're using need language. From there, you can switch to using preference language, such as, "It may be inconvenient, but it's not the end of the world."

> **To say you don't like what's happening in a given situation is far different from saying you can't stand it.**

Life is too short to work yourself into an emotional wreck over common annoyances and setbacks. The apostle Paul discovered this principle. Early in his ministry, he was intense and frequently upset by events. He had a falling out with Barnabas, resented Mark for leaving their ministry and returning home, and differed sharply with some at the church in Jerusalem. Later, however, he was mellower in his relationships, though he was still a man of strong convictions.

In his letter to the Philippians, he specifically addressed the issue of anxiety, telling them that he had "*learned* to be content" (Philippians 4:11, emphasis added). He taught others to center their thought lives on whatever was true and right (Philippians 4:8). He knew full well that the truth sets you free from anxiety and depression (Philippians 4:6–7).

In his second letter to the Corinthians, he explained, "We are hard pressed on every side, but not *crushed*; perplexed, but not in *despair*; persecuted, but not *abandoned*; struck down, but not *destroyed*" (2 Corinthians 4:8–9, emphasis added). Notice that the italicized words are all need language terms. Paul is saying that he learned to be content because he accepted what came his way, as long as it didn't compromise God's Word.

This is what the Bible means by honesty. Certainly, it contributed to the peace Paul described as transcending all understanding (Philippians 4:7). In other words, it's a peace that flatly contradicts the difficulty of the situation.

You can negotiate this path back to mental health with a strategy of purpose:

- By understanding the nature of depression and its usefulness in discovering issues that require your attention, you can change the longstanding habits that have held you back from a better life.

- When you recognize which beliefs are distorting reality, where they came from, and the language you're using to describe present events to yourself because of them, you'll be well on your way to transforming your world.

Your past does not have to determine your present any more than your ill-conceived narratives must shape your future. God's servant Paul came to understand that principle, and so can you.

Eight Things to Remember

It might be useful to summarize, once again, the eight important things you should know as you begin healing:

1 – Depression is actually your ally. Remember that it's an emotional alarm system designed to alert you to problems.

2 – The different patterns of depression can make it challenging to identify. Understanding the gender differences in depression can help you bridge the gap between men and woman and how they respond differently to depression.

3 – Men often disguise depressed feelings with anger or withdrawn stoicism, further isolating them. When upset, rather than act impulsively, respond in a way that won't alienate others and will honestly communicate what you feel.

4 — Many men become depressed when faced with an incapacitating medical condition. Try to find out what you can do with your new limitations instead of giving up.

5 — Some prescribed medications have side effects that include depression. If your depressed feelings are mystifying to you, talk to your doctor.

6 — Distorted understanding of God is toxic to your emotional welfare. Read about scriptural accounts of depressed, godly servants and how God ministered to them.

7 — Though self-disclosure is threatening to many men, recognition of your depression is the first step to recovery. Determine not to live your life in denial, and take the other steps necessary for full liberation.

8 — Carefully examine and dispute your false preconceptions —perhaps with a professional. This can help you finally lay to rest ideas and behaviors that have hindered your life.

These eight things are built on the premise that every experience you have—good or bad—is preparation for the future. You don't have to settle for a cheerless anticipation of the years to come, but rather you can set about beginning to make a difference in the here and now.

And one more thing:

Don't be afraid to seek professional help with your depression.

BIOGRAPHY

Gary H. Lovejoy, MA, MRE, PhD, was a professor of psychology and a professor of religion at Mt. Hood Community College for 32 years and has had a private practice in professional counseling for more than 38 years. He is the founder and current principal therapist of Valley View Counseling Services, LLC in Portland, Oregon.

In addition to earning his doctorate in psychology from United States International University, Dr. Lovejoy also earned a master's degree in religious education from Fuller Theological Seminary. He has taught courses in psychology, world religions, Old Testament, and New Testament.

His years of experience as a counselor have included assisting pastors and ministry leaders. He also counsels individuals, couples, and families dealing with depression, anxiety, conflict resolution, marital issues, and many other issues. He has been a speaker at many family camps, couples' retreats, and college conferences.

Dr. Lovejoy is an evangelical Christian and is presently a member of Athey Creek Christian Fellowship, in West Linn, Oregon. He lives in Happy Valley, Oregon, with his wife, Sue, and has two married adult children and four grandchildren.

We know that men and women are NOT the same.

There are distinct differences between the genders when it comes to depression, too.

Did you know that one in every four women will experience moderate to severe depression? Statistically, depression affects twice as many women as men. The elevated frequency of depression in women is a cause for alarm, particularly since women represent the emotional hub of the home.

It's time to complete the set. The women in your life need **8 Things Every Woman Should Know about Depression.**

Paperback, 112 pages, 4.5 x 6.5 x 0.25 inches.
(ISBN: 9781628624144 — Product Code: 4132X)

www.aspirepress.com

Hope for Those Wrestling with Depression

The *Light in the Darkness Workshop Kit* provides everything you need to lead a group of congregation members through an in-depth study of Dr. Gary Lovejoy and Dr. Gregory Knopf's practical and hopeful book, *Light in the Darkness: Finding Hope in the Shadow of Depression*. It's also a great way to reach out to people in your community who may be experiencing depression. The workshop kit includes:

- 1 *Light in the Darkness: Finding Hope in the Shadow of Depression* book (9780898278255)
- 1 *A Pastor's Guide for the Shadow of Depression* book (9780898278309)
- 1 *Light in the Darkness* DVD (includes 13 video segments, 1 per chapter)
- 1 *Light in the Darkness* Workbook (9780898278286)
- *Light in the Darkness* Group Leader's Guide (free download)

Light in the Darkness Workshop Kit
9780898278279